CATS
SET III

Burmese Cats

Julie Murray
ABDO Publishing Company

visit us at
www.abdopub.com

Published by ABDO Publishing Company, 4940 Viking Drive, Edina, Minnesota 55435.
Copyright © 2003 by Abdo Consulting Group, Inc. International copyrights reserved in
all countries. No part of this book may be reproduced in any form without written
permission from the publisher.

Printed in the United States.

Photo Credits: Animals Animals pp. 11, 15, 17; Corbis pp. 5, 9, 19; Peter Arnold pp. 7, 13;
    Ron Kimball p. 21
Contributing Editors: Tamara L. Britton, Kristin Van Cleaf, Stephanie Hedlund
Book Design & Graphics: Neil Klinepier

Library of Congress Cataloging-in-Publication Data

Murray, Julie, 1969-
    Burmese cats / Julie Murray.
        p. cm. -- (Cats Set III)
    Summary: An introduction to the physical characteristics, personality traits, and history
of the Burmese cat with information on how to choose and care for them as pets.
    ISBN 1-57765-865-5
    1. Burmese cat--Juvenile literature. [1. Burmese cat. 2. Cats. 3. Pets.] I. Title.

SF449.B8 M87 2002
636.8'24--dc21

2002016330

Contents

Lions, Tigers, and Cats

The first cats lived about 35 million years ago. There are several different types of cats. But they all belong to the animal family **Felidae**. There are 38 different species in this family.

Cats are organized into three different categories. Examples of big cats are lions, tigers, jaguars, and leopards. The small cats include **domestic** cats, lynx, and bobcats. Cheetahs are in a group by themselves.

Domestic cats are believed to be the ancestors of the African wildcat. They were tamed about 4,000 years ago in Egypt. Today, there are more than 40 different recognized **breeds** of domestic cats.

Mountain lions are part of the big cat group.

Burmese Cats

The history of the modern Burmese begins about 1930. Dr. Joseph Thompson brought a female cat named Wong Mau to the United States. Wong Mau was from Burma, now called Myanmar, a country in Southeast Asia.

This brown cat was **bred** with a Siamese cat. The male cats of the **litter** were then bred back with Wong Mau. This created a new breed known as the Burmese. Almost all Burmese cats in the United States today can trace their **pedigree** to Wong Mau.

Burmese cats were first recognized as a breed by the **Cat Fanciers' Association (CFA)** in 1936. Cat breeders soon took an interest in the Burmese. They used Siamese cats to expand the breed's numbers.

But many people felt Siamese cats should not be used in Burmese breeding programs. So in 1947, the

CFA withdrew its approval of the Burmese **breed**. The Burmese breeders worked to eliminate the Siamese qualities from their cats. In 1957, the CFA once again gave the Burmese official recognition.

Burmese cats may have been kept by priests in ancient Burma. Modern breeding programs have made the Burmese the breed it is today.

Qualities

Burmese cats have big personalities. They are very active animals. They can be demanding and stubborn at times. Like many cats, they can also be very curious of their environment.

Burmese are also loving cats that like lots of attention. They love to follow their owners around and sit on people's laps. Burmese cats desire company. They do not like to be left alone for long periods of time.

These cats make good family pets. They get along well with children and other animals. Burmese cats are intelligent and adapt well to different living situations.

Burmese cats are playful. They can be taught to do tricks, such as fetching. Their personality is often compared to that of a Siamese.

 Burmese cats have a soft, sweet voice and will often talk with their owners.

Coat and Color

The Burmese has a short coat, with almost no **undercoat**. The coat is **dense** and lies close to the body. The fur is shiny, fine, and satiny.

Most **breed** organizations only recognize certain colors of Burmese for their cat shows. The main colors are sable, champagne, blue, and platinum. Sable is the most common shade.

Burmese of other colors are usually called Foreign, or European Burmese. Colors in this breed may include red, cream, chocolate, brown, and some **tortoiseshell** shades.

Burmese cats' chest and stomach are a lighter color than their back and legs. They usually have yellow to golden eyes. Their nose and paw pads can be brown, gray, or pink.

European Burmese were first bred in the 1960s in England. This European Burmese has a reddish coat and a more wedge-shaped head than a traditional Burmese.

Size

Burmese are medium-sized cats with a rounded body. They are often much heavier than they appear. The average Burmese weighs about eight pounds (4 kg). The males are usually a bit larger than the females.

Burmese cats have strong, muscular bodies with a rounded chest. They have short legs and rounded paw pads. Their medium-length tail tapers toward the end.

Burmese cats have round heads and short, rounded **muzzles**. Their ears are wide at the base and rounded at the tips. The ears are set wide apart on the head and tilt forward slightly. Burmese have large, round eyes set wide apart on their face.

Burmese cats have other names, too. In Germany they are called Burma, and in some English-speaking countries are nicknamed the Burm.

Care

Cats often lick their fur to keep it clean. This grooming also removes loose hairs. Comb Burmese cats with a rubber brush to help keep their fur from knotting up. Occasionally rubbing their coat with a soft **chamois** will keep it glossy.

Like any cat, the Burmese will frequently need to sharpen its claws. This is a natural behavior for all cats. Providing them with a scratching post will save your furniture from damage.

All cats love to play. Movement is important for attracting their attention. So try to provide them with toys they can move with their paws. A ball, **catnip** mouse, or anything movable is good.

It is a natural instinct for cats to bury their waste. So they should be trained to use a **litter box**. The box needs to be cleaned every day. Cats should also be **spayed** or **neutered**, unless you are planning on **breeding** them.

Cats should have regular checkups with a veterinarian. The vet will make sure your cat has the shots and other care it needs to live a long and healthy life.

Feeding

All cats are **carnivores**. They require food that is high in protein, such as meat or fish. Cats can be very picky and do not like changes to their diet.

Homemade diets usually do not provide the **nutrients** that cats need. A better choice is commercial cat food. It comes in three types. They are dry, semidry, and canned. Each kind offers similar nutritional value.

Dry foods are the most convenient. They can prevent **tartar** buildup on your cat's teeth. Canned foods are the most appealing to cats. But they do not stay fresh for very long.

Cats also need fresh water every day. Your cat may love to drink milk. But many cats are unable to **digest** milk. It will often make them sick. Cats also love treats. You can find a variety of treats at your local pet store.

How much to feed your cat depends on how active it is. A playful, outdoor cat will be able to eat more than a calm, indoor cat before becoming overweight.

Kittens

Baby cats are called kittens. Cats are **pregnant** for about 65 days before the kittens are born. Burmese have about five kittens in each **litter**.

All kittens are born blind and helpless. They need to drink their mother's milk for the first three weeks. Then they start to eat solid food. Most kittens stop drinking their mother's milk when they are about eight weeks old.

Kittens start becoming independent when they are about three weeks old. By then they can see, hear, and stand on their own. At about seven weeks, they can run and play. When kittens are 12 weeks old, they can be sold or given away.

Mother cats nurse their kittens for about three weeks. After about six weeks, the mother will encourage her kittens to eat solid food by chasing them away when they come to nurse.

Buying a Kitten

A healthy cat will live about 14 to 16 years. A kitten will become very attached to its owner. So before you buy a kitten, be sure you will be able to take care of it for as long as it lives.

There are many places to get kittens. A qualified **breeder** is the best place to buy a **purebred** kitten. When buying from a breeder, be sure to get the kitten's **pedigree** papers and health records. Pet shelters, veterinarians, and cat shows are also good places to find kittens.

When choosing a kitten, check to see that it is healthy. The ears, nose, mouth, and fur should all be clean. Its eyes should be bright and clear. The kitten should also be alert and playful.

Before bringing your kitten home, set out food and water dishes, a litter box, and some toys. Also make sure you're not allergic to cat fur!

Glossary

breed - a group of cats that shares the same appearance and characteristics. A breeder is a person who raises cats. Raising cats is often called breeding them.

carnivore - an animal or plant that eats meat.

Cat Fanciers' Association (CFA) - a group that sets the standards for breeds of cats.

catnip - the dried leaves and stems of a plant in the mint family. Catnip is used as a stuffing in cat toys because some cats are attracted to its strong smell.

chamois - a soft, pliable leather or cloth.

dense - having many pieces in a small area.

digest - to break down food in the stomach.

domestic - animals that are tame.

Felidae - the Latin name for the cat family.

litter - all of the kittens born at one time to a mother cat.

litter box - a box where cats dispose of their waste.

muzzle - an animal's nose and jaws.

neuter - to remove a male animal's reproductive organs.

nutrients - vitamins and minerals that all living things need to survive.

pedigree - a record of an animal's ancestors.

pregnant - having one or more babies growing within the body.

purebred - an animal whose parents are both from the same breed.

spay - to remove a female animal's reproductive organs.

tartar - a crust that forms on the teeth. Tartar is made of saliva, food particles, and salts.

tortoiseshell - a color pattern of blotches of black, orange, and cream.

undercoat - soft, short hair or fur that is partly covered by longer protective hairs.

Web Sites

Would you like to learn more about Burmese cats? Please visit **www.abdopub.com** to find up-to-date Web site links about cat care and the Burmese breed. These links are routinely monitored and updated to provide the most current information available.

Index